Hear It and Sing It!

EXPLORING MODAL JAZZ

JUDY NIEMACK

To access audio, visit:
www.halleonard.com/mylibrary

Enter Code
2401-3396-6300-2464

SECOND FLOOR MUSIC

EXCLUSIVELY DISTRIBUTED BY

HAL•LEONARD®
7777 W. BLUEMOUND RD. P.O. BOX 13819 MILWAUKEE, WI 53213

ISBN 978-0-634-08099-9

A DON SICKLER PRODUCTION

Hear It and Sing It!

Exploring Modal Jazz

JUDY NIEMACK

AUDIO TRACK LISTING

All of the track numbers listed below can be accessed online: you'll find your individual code number on the opening Title page. The audio tracks begin with seven vocal warm-up tracks. I've sung a few examples at the beginning of each one to get you started. The remaining tracks demonstrate the modes and modal workouts. Tracks labeled with white track numbers in black boxes indicate my vocal examples of the modes and modal workouts. These are followed by the same tracks, shown with black numbers in white boxes, without my voice, where you can experiment and practice improvising on your own.

Vocal Warm-up Tracks

1 **Warm-up I**
2 **Warm-up 2**
3 **Warm-up 3**
4 **Warm-up 4**
5 **Warm-up 5**
6 **Warm-up 6**
7 **Warm-up 7**

Modal Jazz Tracks

8 **Ionian mode** (page 40)
Ionian workout
9 **Intervals**
10 **Thirds**
11 **Triads**
12 **Call and response**
Rhythm section alone
13 **Ionian mode**
14 **Your Ionian workout**

15 **Dorian mode** (page 44)
Dorian workout
16 **Intervals**
17 **Thirds**
18 **Triads**
19 **Call and response**
Rhythm section alone
20 **Dorian mode**
21 **Your Dorian workout**

22 **Phrygian mode** (page 48)
Phrygian workout
23 **Intervals**
24 **Thirds**
25 **Triads**
26 **Call and response**
Rhythm section alone
27 **Phrygian mode**
28 **Your Phrygian workout**

29 **Lydian mode** (page 52)
Lydian workout
30 **Intervals**
31 **Thirds**
32 **Triads**
33 **Call and response**
Rhythm section alone
34 **Lydian mode**
35 **Your Lydian workout**

36 **Mixolydian mode** (page 56)
Mixolydian workout
37 **Intervals**
38 **Thirds**
39 **Triads**
40 **Call and response**
Rhythm section alone
41 **Mixolydian mode**
42 **Your Mixolydian workout**

43 **Aeolian mode** (page 60)
Aeolian workout
44 **Intervals**
45 **Thirds**
46 **Triads**
47 **Call and response**
Rhythm section alone
48 **Aeolian mode**
49 **Your Aeolian workout**

50 **Locrian mode** (page 64)
Locrian workout
51 **Intervals**
52 **Thirds**
53 **Triads**
54 **Call and response**
Rhythm section alone
55 **Locrian mode**
56 **Your Locrian workout**

Total Audio time: 01:11:04

Tip: You can play combinations of tracks or to repeat tracks for your convenience. For example, you can hear all the modes sung in sequence (8 15 22 29 36 43 50), sing all the modes alone with the rhythm section (13 20 27 34 41 48 55), or hear triads sung with all the modes (11 18 25 32 39 46 53).

INTRODUCTION

There's a wonderful line Billie Holiday sang back in the 1930s:

> Oh, you can go to the East, go to the West,
> but someday you'll come, weary at heart,
> back where you started from.
> "Back in Your Own Backyard," Jolson, Rose & Dryer

When I began singing jazz, I loved Ella Fitzgerald's style and wanted to be able to scat like she did. At first I improvised by ear, and my success depended on my inspiration and familiarity with the song. But as time went on, I began to feel limited. I was repeating myself, and I wanted to expand my musical vocabulary. Friends of mine were taking lessons in improvisation with a great jazz saxophonist, Warne Marsh, and suggested that I study with him, too. He agreed to take me as his first vocal student.

As I studied the theoretical side of music, and put the concepts he showed me into practice, I found it both fascinating and liberating. I discovered that to develop one's musical vocabulary and improvisational skills, some knowledge of music theory was essential. But all the theoretical training in the world was useless if I couldn't *hear* it, and I had to hear it to be able to sing it. So in practicing, I focused on each chord and scale separately, teaching myself to be aware of which note I was singing. Then I worked on chord progressions and practiced improvising over them very slowly. When it came time to perform, I still improvised by ear, but gradually the new things I had been practicing appeared in my scat solos.

Learning by repetition is an age-old method, and while it's especially effective in vocal improvisation, it's also essential to becoming an accomplished instrumental improviser. Warne showed me how instrumentalists transcribe recorded solos by ear and learn to sing and play them. Even the great saxophonist Charlie Parker transcribed solos by other players.

> The records were Charlie's most important subject for
> study. . . . He slowly committed each of the Lester Young
> solos to memory. He hummed and sang them to himself.
> Ross Russell, *Bird Lives!*

Much of Western music is based on the seven modes of the major scale: Ionian, Dorian, Phrygian, Lydian, Mixolydian, Aeolian and Locrian. The ancient Greeks named them after various deities and cities. In medieval times, Christian monks switched around some of the Greek names when they wrote them down, and the names as the monks recorded them are still used today.

Studying these modes is useful for understanding (and passing) music theory courses in both the classical and jazz disciplines. But jazz improvisers in particular must understand them thoroughly because each mode is used with one or more chords found in the standard jazz repertoire. With *Hear It and Sing It!* you'll become familiar with the "color" of each chord and the mode it implies, preparing you to move on to chord progressions.

Students often tell me that the hardest part of practicing is getting started. With this book, getting started is simple: whether you're in your practice room, in your hot tub, or driving your car, just play the tracks from the beginning and sing along. (Of course, the most effective way to practice singing is to simply stand with good posture and sing, but many people spend a lot of time in the car, and it's another opportunity to practice.)

I chose a great New York jazz rhythm section to accompany me, so that the grooves would be there from the start. (Our pianist is Bruce Barth, our bassist is Dennis Irwin and drummer Kenny Washington completes the trio.) After the eight-minute warm-up, which combines ear training with basic vocal exercises, you'll hear me singing practice patterns and call-and-response ideas for improvising in each of the seven modes. Following the modal workout tracks are tracks by just the rhythm section, which give you space to try improvising on your own.

This book, written to accompany the Audio Tracks, begins with instructions for singing the warm-up exercises. There follows an introduction to music theory and the structure and functions of chords. I then discuss the seven modes of the major scale and their uses in jazz harmony. The next chapter includes a short history of the evolution of scat syllables, with suggestions for developing your own vocabulary of syllables. Finally, you'll find all of the modal workouts transcribed, so that you can read them as you sing along and simultaneously improve your sight-singing.

After twenty-five years of practicing, performing and teaching vocal jazz, I've come back where I started from. Learning by ear is still the most important part of becoming a better improviser. I designed *Hear It and Sing It!* as a fun and effective way to improve your vocal technique and internalize the basic scales used in jazz.

But don't worry about the theory yet. Just play the audio, listen and sing!

WARM-UPS

These exercises are designed to get you in shape and in the mood to sing. I strongly recommend doing warm-ups every day before you begin your practice session. After you've sung along with this eight-minute workout, you'll be ready to practice with the following tracks or work on your repertoire without straining your voice. Some days you may want to repeat an exercise, or the whole warm-up, depending on your physical condition—late nights, vocal fatigue or a cold will naturally affect your requirements. If an exercise is uncomfortable, causes strain, or is too high or low to sing easily, drop out at that point. If you have already warmed up, skip ahead to the track with the mode of your choice.

At the beginning of each warm-up track, I've sung a few examples to get you started. Continue on your own when my voice drops out.

Track 1. For the first exercise, we'll start with a hum, using a relaxed, light sound. Try gradually dropping your jaw as you sing the five-note scale to create more room for the lower notes. Feel the buzzing in your lips and teeth. You can also try "chewing" the sound as you sing, as if you had a piece of gum in your mouth, This will help relax the jaw and tongue.

1   **Medium swing**

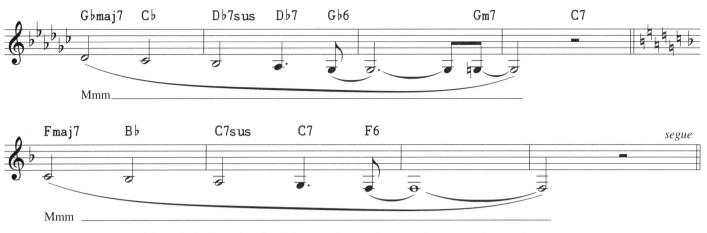

Track 2. For the "ooh" vowel on this exercise, round your lips,
pursing them slightly (as if you're about to be kissed), then drop your jaw
slightly, creating a cavern in your mouth where the "ooh" can resonate.

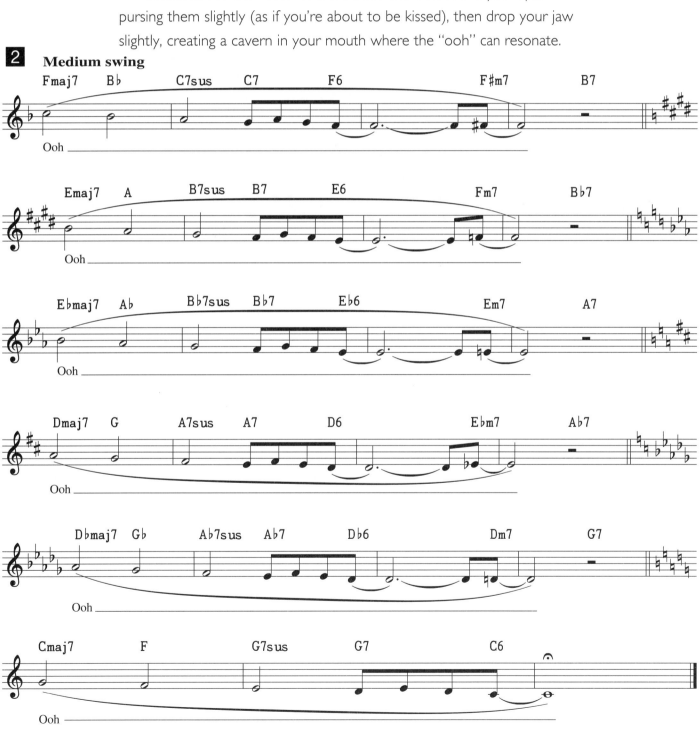

Track 3. This exercise begins with a hum to create what's called "forward placement" of the tone in the middle register of the voice. Next, open your mouth with the lips relaxed, singing the exercise on "ee" and feeling the vowel sound right behind the teeth. Finally, sing the same five notes on "ooh," bringing the bright, forward resonance of the "ee" into the "ooh" sound. For some people, this exercise is more comfortable when it starts with an "n." Try both "m" and "n" and see which feels best for you. For women, this exercise should be done in head voice, as if you were singing a classical vocal exercise. Sing it lightly!

3   **Even eighth notes**

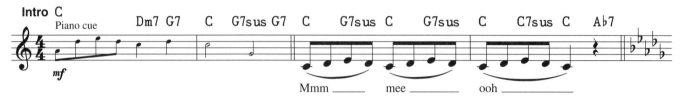

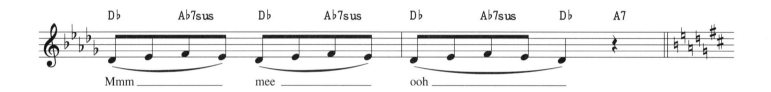

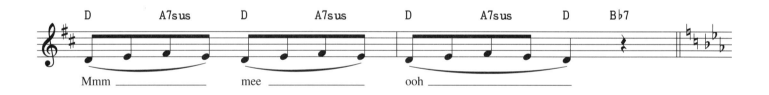

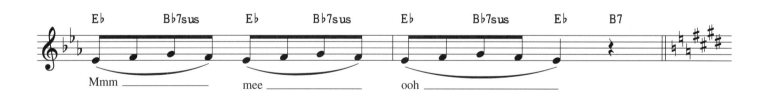

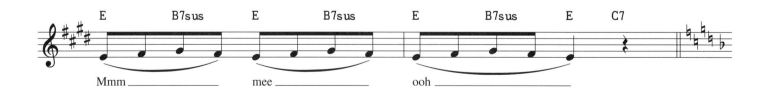

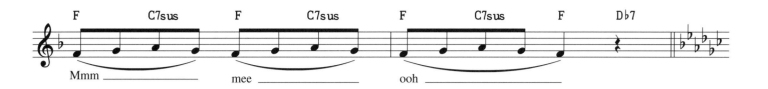

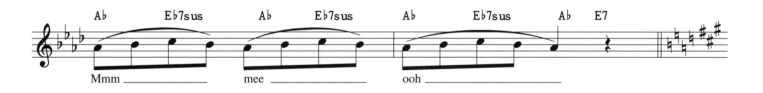

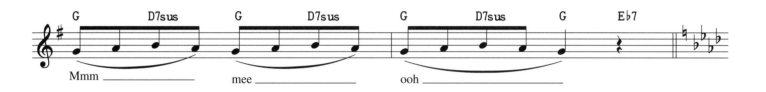

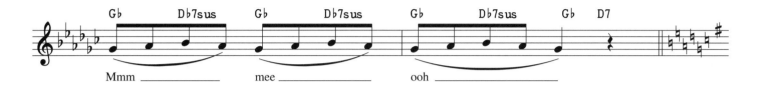

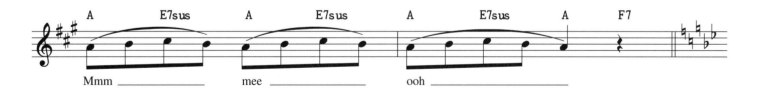

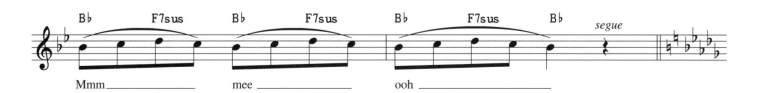

Track 4. On this exercise, we'll sing the first, second, third, fourth, fifth and seventh degrees of the Aeolian mode, also called the natural or pure minor scale. Notice how it feels to sing the minor third and minor seventh as opposed to the major third and major seventh we usually sing in warm-ups. Using the Italian rolled "r" on this exercise helps to bring the tone forward. If you can't roll your "r"s, begin with an "m." Try to focus the "ooh" and "oh" in the same place in your mouth as the "ee" vowel. This will bring the ringing overtones of the "ee" into the darker "ooh" and "oh" vowels.

4   **Even eighth notes**

Ree _____ roo _____ roh _____

Ree _____ roo _____ roh _____

Ree _____ roo _____ roh _____

Ree _____ roo _____ roh _____

Ree _____ roo _____ roh _____

Ree _____ roo _____ roh _____

segue

Ree _____ roo _____ roh _____

Track 5. Like track 4, this exercise is in minor. It combines staccato arpeggios with legato scales. It can be tricky to negotiate ascending scales, but with practice it will become as easy as singing descending scales. Imagine an "h" before each of the staccato notes, and relax your abdomen after each attack. Keep your sound light and bouncy, as though you're bouncing a balloon. Sing the legato runs like water flowing in a clear, bubbling brook (or create your own mental images to keep it light and flowing).

5 **Even eighth notes**

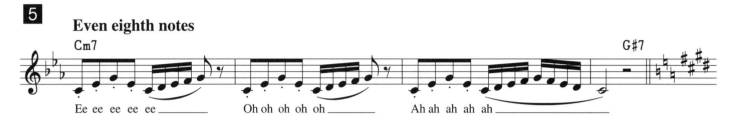

Ee ee ee ee ee _____   Oh oh oh oh oh _____   Ah ah ah ah ah _____

Ee ee ee ee ee _____   Oh oh oh oh oh _____   Ah ah ah ah ah _____

Ee ee ee ee ee _____   Oh oh oh oh oh _____   Ah ah ah ah ah _____

Ee ee ee ee ee _____   Oh oh oh oh oh _____   Ah ah ah ah ah _____

Ee ee ee ee ee _____   Oh oh oh oh oh _____   Ah ah ah ah ah _____

Ee ee ee ee ee _____   Oh oh oh oh oh _____   Ah ah ah ah ah _____

Ee ee ee ee ee _____   Oh oh oh oh oh _____   Ah ah ah ah ah _____

Ee ee ee ee ee _____   Oh oh oh oh oh _____   Ah ah ah ah ah _____

Ee ee ee ee ee _____   Oh oh oh oh oh _____   Ah ah ah ah ah _____

Track 6. On the following page is an exercise for increasing the flexibility and speed of the tongue. I used a minor scale with a major seventh, or harmonic minor scale, on this one. When you sing the "l"s, limit the action to the tip of the tongue. To check for excess jaw motion, lightly place your index finger on the center of your chin as you sing. Your chin shouldn't move.

Track 7. This last exercise combines ear training with flexibility and range extension using an arpeggiated major seventh and then a major ninth chord. (You don't have to understand it right now; just hear it and sing it.) Some people find it easier to reach the higher notes using "see-ooh."

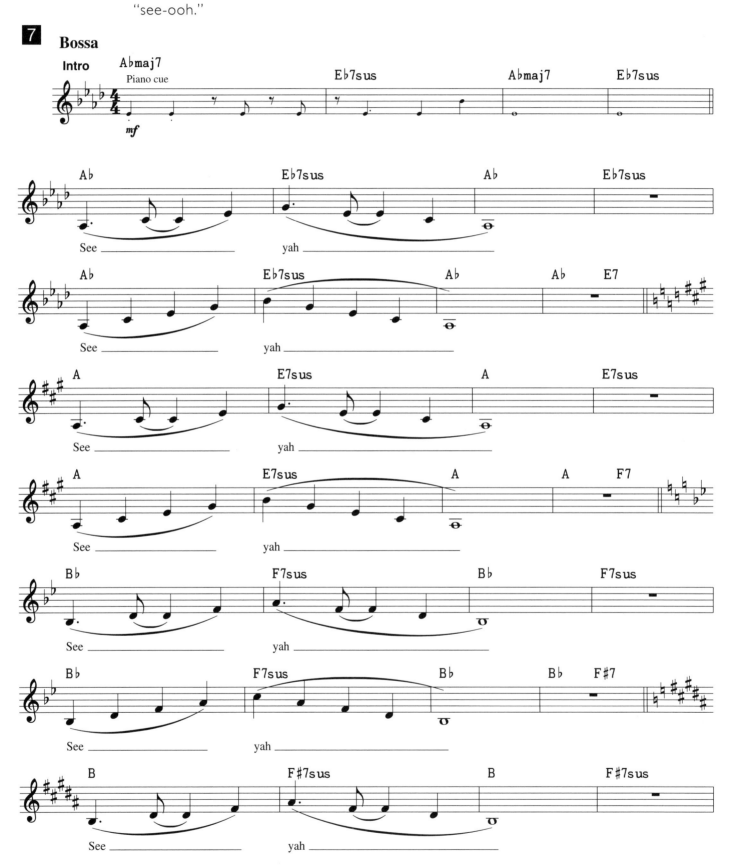

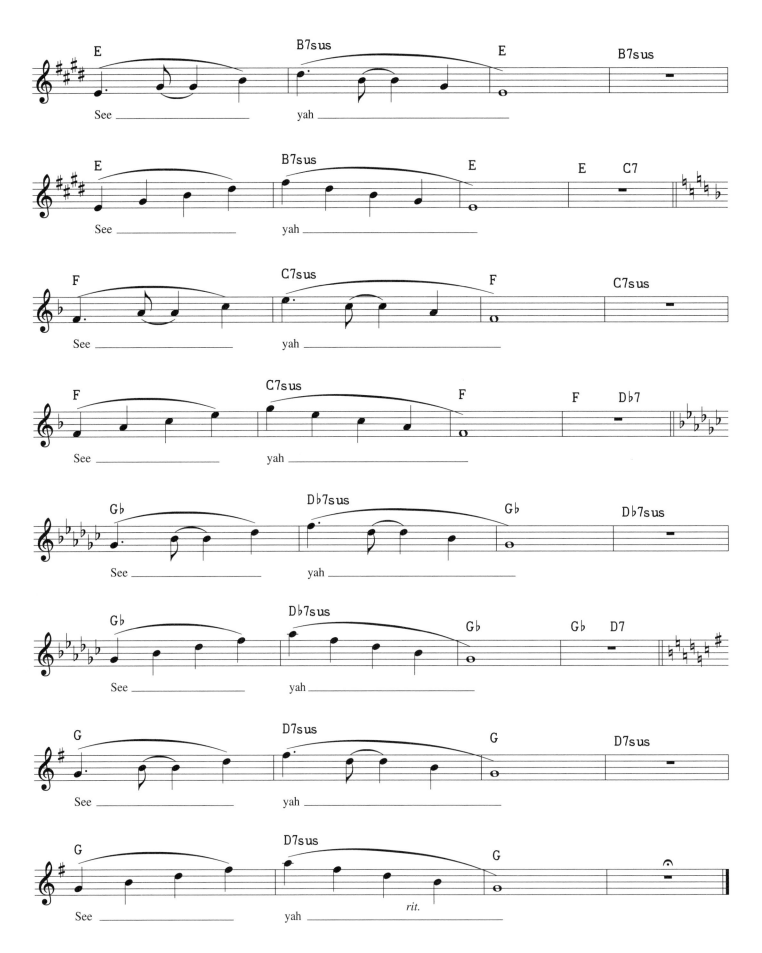

Now you are warmed up and ready for the next adventure: the modes
of the major scale. Have fun!

THE CREATORS OF MODAL JAZZ

From the beginnings of jazz, each generation of musicians has challenged the boundaries of harmony, melody and rhythm. When a new style is born, it inspires heated debate over "What is jazz?" With each new phase the music moves in a new direction, pushed by the artists' drive to find an original sound.

As linear as this may sound, jazz doesn't fall into neat stylistic packages. Each new style creates currents that flow out in many directions, all seeking truth, for a real personal expression. Modal jazz was one of the waves that developed in the 1950s, as a result of and in reaction to bebop, the music that preceded it.

Bebop, so called after the syllables used in scat singing, developed during the mid–1940s and early 1950s, created by jazz musicians such as trumpeter Dizzy Gillespie, pianists Bud Powell and Thelonious Monk, and saxophonist Charlie Parker. It was pronounced revolutionary, and provoked outrage and arguments about what "real" jazz was. The big band era was fading, and soloists were performing in small jazz clubs with their own smaller ensembles. For the first time, the role of the music changed from a soundtrack for dancing and social events to a hip modern-day chamber music. With bebop, jazz fans came to sit and listen.

The beboppers were virtuoso instrumentalists with a genius for melodic invention. They cultivated flexibility, range and speed, favoring eighth-note lines often played at extremely fast tempos. They added alternate chord changes and upper-structure harmonies to existing chord progressions to make them more interesting and challenging for improvisation. Their music built upon and reacted to the New Orleans and swing styles of their predecessors, becoming more complex and exciting.

The trumpeter Miles Davis moved to New York in 1944, ostensibly to attend the Juilliard School of Music, but actually to find his hero, Charlie Parker. Although Davis spent few days in school, he managed to complete a year and a half of musical studies, but soon devoted himself to trying to join Parker's band. He succeeded, and spent several years playing bebop with his idol.

Several years before Davis's arrival in New York, the composer and arranger Gil Evans had joined the Claude Thornhill Band. Evans brought new instrumentation to the big band, using French horns and tuba, achieving the orchestral sound that became his trademark. His scores were "orchestral improvisations" based on popular songs or works by such composers as Charlie Parker and Modest Moussorgsky. He later collaborated with Miles Davis on the *Birth of the Cool* recordings (1949–50) and wrote and arranged for him on *Miles Ahead* (1957), *Porgy and Bess* (1959) and *Sketches of Spain* (1960).

In 1945, a young drummer and struggling composer named George Russell moved to New York City. Fascinated by classical music and searching for an approach to jazz improvisation that would allow greater freedom, he became an influence on the jazz scene. Russell developed a theory of scales and modes that was published in 1953 as *The Lydian Chromatic Concept of Tonal Organization*.

Pianist Bill Evans, also living in New York at the time, studied with George Russell and introduced him to Miles in 1948. Although Evans's own compositions were for the most part not modal, he has come to represent that style of playing because he provided the harmonic background for Miles Davis. In 1959, the two collaborated on Miles' *Kind of Blue*, featuring the more relaxed and introspective music later to be called modal jazz.

At the outset of the 1950s another wave was building, one that would wash over jazz during the next decade. Miles Davis, along with the pianist John Lewis and the composer and arranger Gil Evans, were studious types, learning classical compositional methods. They formed a cadre of musical sensibility that used bebop conventions as a springboard, adding ideas gleaned from their classical studies. They codified what had happened in bebop, and discussed harmonic and melodic possibilities with other composers.

Pianist John Lewis joined Dizzy Gillespie's bop-style big band in 1946, and developed his skills as a composer and arranger there and at the Manhattan School of Music. He later became the pianist and musical director of the Modern Jazz Quartet, an ensemble that lasted for twenty years. He wrote a number of third-stream works combining European compositional techniques and jazz improvisation.

Over the course of the 1950s and early 1960s these musicians moved into the foreground. They wanted to improvise not only over the rapid-fire chord progressions of bebop, but also languidly, developing ideas over many measures of one mode or chord, experimenting with slowing the harmonic rhythm, or pace, at which the chords progress. It's been said that bebop is like walking into a house and exploring every room, from the basement to attic. In modal jazz you find the most comfortable room, and just hang out there.

As bebop developed its virtuosic, complex of chord changes, it acquired certain clichés. John Coltrane's "Giant Steps" is one example. The changes go by so quickly that it is difficult to improvise a melodic line that flows horizontally through the harmonies; most players resort to a series of patterns that fit each chord.

The next wave of jazz musicians wanted to break out of those patterns, concentrating more on individual expression. But many swing and bebop veterans were uncomfortable with the unresolved, "open" quality of the new compositions.

Rather than 32-bar tunes with two chord changes per measure, as in the beboppers' favorite "I Got Rhythm," they favored tunes in long sections of one chord or mode, often with a repeated figure in the bass line, or sections with vamps (short repeated chord progressions). One chord might be played for as many as 24 bars, leaving space for melodic exploration. (If you play the last eight and first 16 bars of "So What" by Miles Davis, or "Impressions" by John Coltrane, you'll find 24 bars of D Dorian mode over which to improvise.) Jazz musicians began to think of chords as horizontal (scalar) rather than vertical (chordal).

Miles Davis's "Milestones" was the first jazz tune based on modes to be widely known. He recorded it on the album of the same name, released in 1958. "Milestones" has a 32-bar A-A-B-A structure, in which the A section uses a G Dorian mode (with an emphasized C in the bass), and the B section the Aeolian mode on A.

Miles' next recording, *Kind of Blue* (1959), brought modal jazz into the mainstream. It included such modal classics as "So What" and "Flamenco Sketches," as well as two of his blues compositions, "All Blues" and "Freddie Freeloader." It has since sold more than five million copies, becoming one of the best-selling jazz recordings of all time.

Modal jazz has survived the test of time and is here to stay. It has become part of the hip-hop, drum and bass, and pop musical vocabulary as the waves set in motion in the 1940s influence the music of today.

THEORY BASICS

Before beginning to study the modes, you'll need to understand the building blocks of music. If you have some background in music theory, you may want to skip ahead to the "Modes" section (page 32).

INTERVALS

An interval is simply the distance in pitch, or the space on a musical staff, between two notes.

Understanding intervals is the first step in understanding music theory. It's also helpful in transposing chords and melodies, something jazz vocalists must do to write lead sheets in their most comfortable keys.

Understanding and hearing intervals is even more important for a vocal improviser than for an instrumentalist. When your voice is the instrument, you depend on your ear to distinguish the notes that sound best with the chords you are hearing. Since you have no strings to pluck or keys to play, you can't determine what to sing by sensation or sight; you have to hear it.

Whole and half steps (tones and semitones)

Intervals are measured by the number of half or whole steps between them. In Western music, the smallest difference in pitch between one note and the next is traditionally a half step, or semitone. Two half steps equal one whole step, or tone. A whole step is also called a major second.

Here is the chromatic scale (ascending and descending), which consists entirely of half steps. This scale includes all the white and black keys in one octave (such as C to C) on the piano. There are 12 half steps in an octave.

Chromatic scale

Here is the whole tone scale (ascending and descending), consisting entirely of whole steps. There are six whole steps in an octave.

Whole tone scale

Types of intervals

We can think of an interval in two ways: as the number of whole and/ or half steps between two notes, or as a combination of two smaller intervals. For example, a perfect fifth contains seven half steps, or three and one-half whole steps; or it can be thought of as a major third plus a minor third.

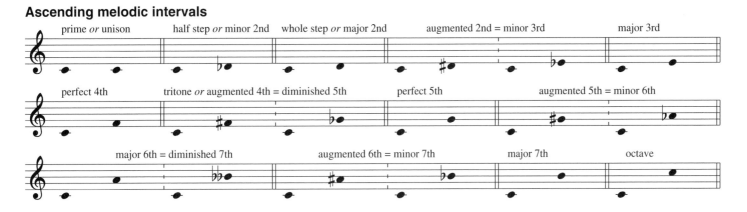

There are two kinds of intervals, melodic and harmonic. Melodic intervals consist of two tones sounded one after the other; harmonic intervals are two tones sounded simultaneously. Thus, intervals are found in both horizontal (melodic) and vertical (harmonic or chordal) structures.

Table of intervals

Melodic interval   **Harmonic interval**

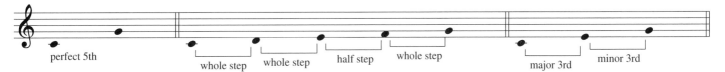

This table shows all the melodic intervals, from the half step to the octave. They are shown from middle C to C an octave above. Some intervals have several names. The most commonly used name is given first.

It is important be able to hear and sing each interval downward, which

Ascending melodic intervals

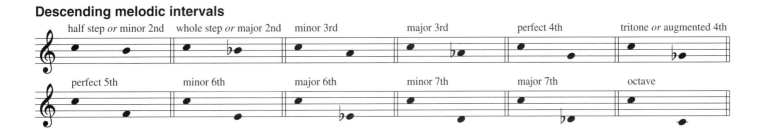

is more difficult, as well as upward. This table shows the twelve intervals from C above middle C down to middle C.

Descending melodic intervals

Intervals larger than an octave

When we pass the octave point in the scale, we continue to number the notes sequentially through the next octave. Intervals larger than an octave span an octave and a smaller interval. A second sounded an octave above the root, or tonic note, of the chord is called a ninth; a third is called a tenth; a fourth an eleventh, etc.

Here are some commonly used intervals larger than an octave:

Note: It's important to be able to sing every interval in each of the scales you study. When you practice with the audio, you will notice that for each mode, I have sung the seven diatonic intervals (see below) from the root to the root an octave above, and then descending from the root an octave above to each interval below. When you sing along with this section, be aware of which interval you are singing. For example, when you sing C, D, C, think "Root, major second, root."

Diatonic melodies or chords include only the notes of a given scale. For example, in the C major scale, diatonic chords and melodies use only the white keys on the piano. In the F major scale, diatonic chords and melodies use only F, G, A, B♭ C, D and E.

BUILDING CHORDS

A chord consists of three or more notes sounded at once. Usually, chords are built in thirds, using alternating notes of the scale. Each scale degree is denoted by an Arabic numeral (1, 2, 3, 4, etc.), which shows the note's melodic position in the scale.

Triads

A triad is the simplest, most basic chord. It consists of three tones, usually alternating tones of the scale, such as the first tone, the third and the fifth. The bottom tone is called the root; the others are a third and fifth above the root. There are four basic combinations of major and minor thirds that form the four basic triads.

Most everyone can sing the major triad, which consists of the first, third and fifth notes of a major scale, or do, mi and sol. It can be thought of as two thirds stacked up, with a major third on the bottom and a minor third on top.

The minor triad consists of the first, third and fifth notes of a minor scale. It can also be created by lowering the third of the major triad by a half step, or by stacking up a minor third on the bottom and a major third on top.

An augmented triad is a major triad where the fifth is raised a half step. A diminished triad is a minor triad where the fifth is lowered a half step.

Five types of triads are commonly used in jazz. The first four—major, minor, diminished and augmented—are built up from the root in thirds.

The fifth triad is called the sus4 chord, which is a major or minor triad in which the third scale step is replaced by the fourth, thereby suspending its resolution. Although in classical music the fourth would normally resolve to the third, in jazz and pop music the "unsettled" sound of the suspended fourth is familiar and comfortable to the ear, and sus chords are common.

Sixth and seventh chords

The chords most often used in jazz are sixth and seventh chords.

Sixth chords are formed by adding the sixth scale degree to a triad. A major sixth chord is a major triad with the sixth scale step from the major scale added. A minor sixth chord is a minor triad with the same sixth scale step as in the major sixth chord.

Five types of seventh chords are commonly used: major, dominant, minor, half-diminished and diminished. This chart shows three ways of conceiving seventh chords: building the interval structure; using the tones of a major scale; and adding a seventh scale tone to a triad.

Type of 7th chord	Interval structure	Tones of major scale	Triad + 7th
major	maj3, m3, maj3	1, 3, 5, 7	major triad + major 7th
dominant	maj3, m3, m3	1, 3, 5, ♭7	major triad + minor 7th
minor	m3, maj3, m3	1, ♭3, 5, ♭7	minor triad + minor 7th
half-diminished	m3, m3, maj3	1, ♭3, ♭5, ♭7	diminished triad + minor 7th
diminished	m3, m3, m3	1, ♭3, ♭5, ♭♭7	diminished triad + diminished 7th

Here are some alterations, or changed notes, found in seventh chords commonly used in jazz:

Major and dominant chords may be augmented by raising the fifth degree.

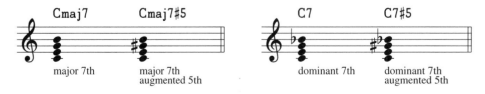

A minor seventh chord can be altered by raising the seventh degree.

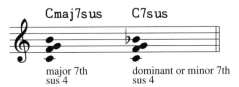

Major, minor and dominant seventh chords may also contain a suspended fourth.

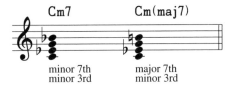

Larger chord structures: Extensions

As we have learned, seventh chords are built using the odd-numbered scale tones: 1, 3, 5 and 7. Continuing up the scale, still using the odd-numbered scale tones, the ninth, eleventh and thirteenth of the chord follow. These are called extensions of the chord. They are commonly used with seventh chords to add interesting musical color. The extensions may also be altered, using, for example, the ♭9, ♯9, ♯11, and ♭13.

A major ninth chord is made up of the first, third, fifth, seventh and ninth notes of a major scale, or 1, 3, 5, 7, 9.

The largest chords generally used in jazz are thirteenth chords. Since the fifteenth note of a scale is a repetition of the root, or first note of the scale, extensions beyond the thirteenth are not usually added.

Thirteenth chords consist of seven notes, or all the notes in a scale. Remember that the ninth is the same note as the second, the eleventh the same as the fourth, and the thirteenth the same as the sixth.

Because in a major scale the fourth (or eleventh) sounds dissonant, when adding extensions to a major seventh chord, the eleventh is usually raised (♯11).

Chord and scale relationships

As we've discovered, chords can be built in thirds on each note of a scale. Here are the seven diatonic seventh chords that can be built on the notes of the C major scale.

Chords are often labeled with Roman numerals denoting their relation to the chord's root to describe their function in the harmonic progression.

Chord functions

After learning how to build chords, a jazz improviser must understand how they are used in chord progressions—how each chord progresses to the next (function) and which chords can substitute for each other to create different effects (substitution). Each type of chord has a harmonic tendency to progress to another specific chord, and therefore has a certain function within the chord progression. Chords that function in the same way may substitute for each other.

Tonic and dominant

A triad built on the first note of the scale, or tonic, is called the tonic chord. It is the main chord of the piece, the most stable and conclusive. Traditionally, the tonic chord was used to begin and end a composition.

The next in importance is the dominant chord, the triad built on the fifth note of the major scale. It sets up tension that is resolved by the tonic chord. The progression from dominant to tonic gives a strong sense of conclusion, which is why it is often used at the end of a phrase, melody or composition.

For the purpose of our study of the modes of the major scale, here are the basic functions of the diatonic chords in major shown above:

Imaj7   The **Imaj7** chord can be thought of as home, as it establishes the key center. Most progressions begin and end on this chord. It tends not to progress to another chord, but it can lead anywhere.

IIm7   The **IIm7** chord substitutes for the **IVmaj7**. It tends to progress to **V** (down a fifth) or to ♭**II** (down a half step).

IIIm7   The IIIm7 chord substitutes for Imaj7. It progresses to VIm7 (down a fifth), or to ♭III (down a half step).

IVmaj7   The IVmaj7 chord substitutes for the IIm7. In classical music theory it progresses to V. In jazz tunes, it often goes to IIIm7, IVm6 or Imaj7. Because it is a major7 chord, it can also serve as the Imaj7 (or tonic chord) in a temporary key center in a song.

V7   The V7 chord usually progresses down a fifth to Imaj7.

VIm7   The VIm7 chord progresses down a fifth to IIm7, or down a half step to ♭VI. It is also the key center of the relative minor (see Aeolian mode).

VIIm7♭5   The VIIm7♭5 chord substitutes for V7, and progresses to I.

I hope this short summary of music theory for jazz improvisation motivates you to further study with one of the many jazz theory books available. For a deeper understanding of chords and harmony, I recommend:

The Jazz Language by Dan Haerle (Warner Brothers Publications)
The Jazz Theory Book by Mark Levine (Sher Music Co.)
Vocal Improvisation by Michele Weir (Advance Music)

THE MODES

The definition of a mode is "a scale derived from or generated by another scale."

Although we are accustomed to hearing a major scale sung from its root (first degree) to the root an octave above, there are several other manners, or modes, in which it can be sung. Each mode is created by beginning on a different degree of a major scale and moving up the scale to the same note an octave above. All seven modes of the major scale contain the same notes, but each has a different starting point. The major scale from which each is derived is called the parent scale.

As you listen to and sing along with the audio tracks, you will notice that although they consist of the same notes as the parent scales, each mode has a unique musical color.

It's easy to find each of the modes by playing only the white keys of the piano from C to C, from D to D, from E to E, and so on.

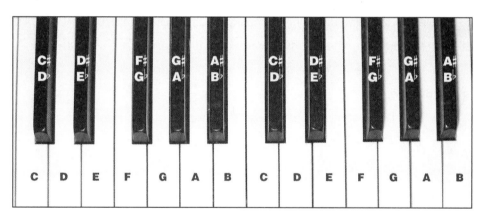

Scale degree	Name of mode	Location on piano's white keys
I	Ionian	C to C
2	Dorian	D to D
3	Phrygian	E to E
4	Lydian	F to F
5	Mixolydian	G to G
6	Aeolian	A to A
7	Locrian	B to B

It is helpful to think of modes in three ways. The first is to see the mode in relation to the parent scale from which it is derived. Here are the modes of the major scale in C. Therefore, C major is the parent scale.

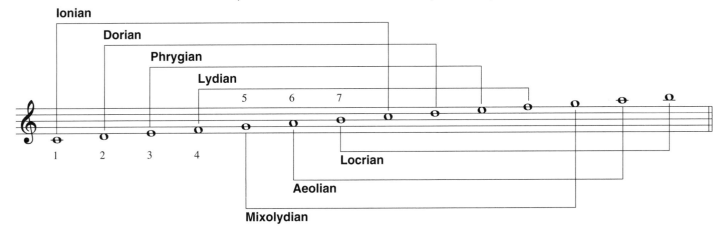

The second way is to learn the modes as a sequence of half steps and whole steps. As in the major scale, there are two half steps and five whole steps in each mode, but as the starting note shifts, the pattern of whole and half steps also shifts.

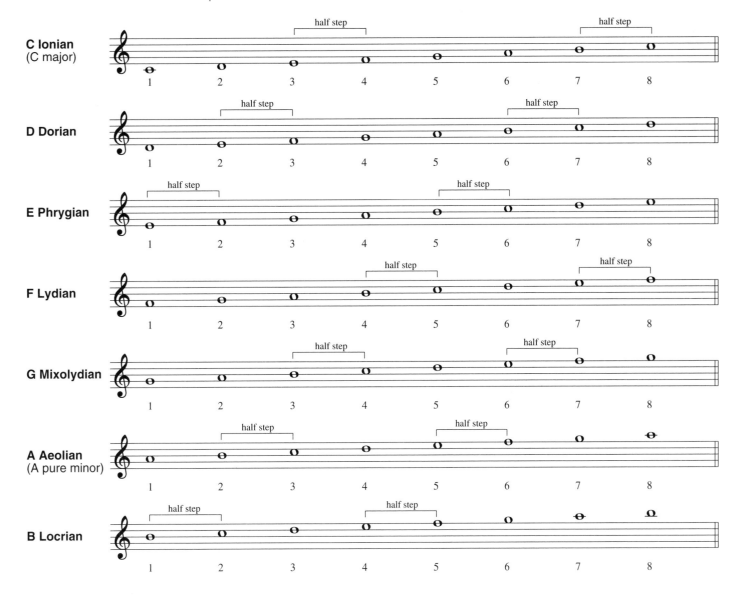

The third way to look at the modes is in comparison to a major
(Ionian) scale:

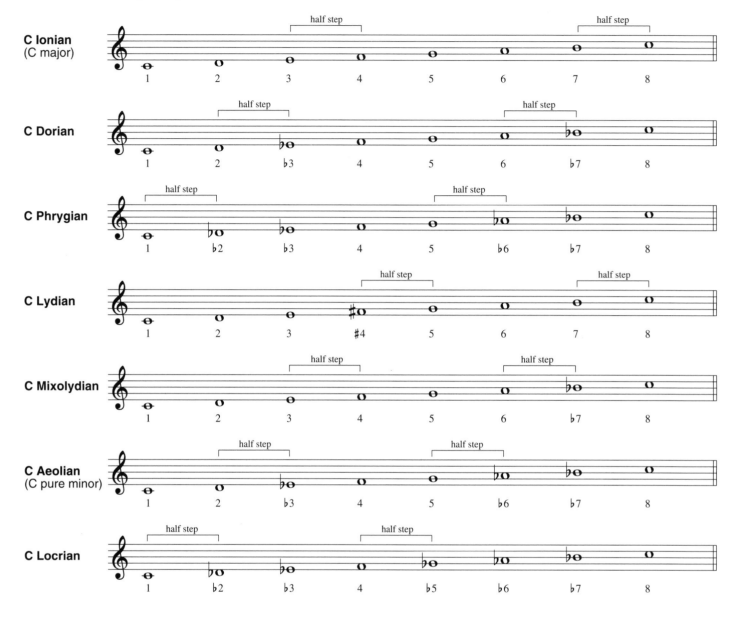

SCAT SYLLABLES

The tradition of "scat singing," or wordless improvisation, dates back to the 1920s. It began as a vocal imitation of the sounds made by saxophones, trumpets and trombones, which were (of course!) an extension of the human voice. But it didn't end there. The language of scat is still evolving, as jazz singers from various countries bring the syllables and sounds of their own languages into their scat vocabularies.

The originators of scat singing were jazz instrumentalists who sang their improvised solos as well as played them. They projected their own playing into their vocals without actually imitating their instruments, and the attack and inflections of their instrumental solos were reflected in their choice of syllables. For example, the first scat singers in the 1920s and 1930s used syllables that came from the tonguing used by trumpet and trombone players, called "doodle tonguing." For trumpet players, scat singing was a chance for them to rest their "chops," or their lips, in the course of a long evening of playing.

The most famous scat legend is that Louis Armstrong accidentally dropped his music while recording the pop tune "Heebie Jeebies" with his group, the Hot Five, and like the true professional he was, continued singing, inventing his own nonsense syllables. The tune was a hit, and "scatting" became a household word. Louis's scat choruses are as brilliant as his trumpet solos and as full of humor as his gravelly vocals. His incredible melodic sense and deeply swinging time provide a lesson in essential jazz vocabulary for all aspiring scat singers.

Certain combinations of syllables evoke particular eras of jazz. "Vo dee oh do" brings back the nasal "Radio Days" style of the 1920s. The 1930s brought a host of new nonsense syllables to the scat lexicon. The hook in Duke Ellington's "It Don't Mean a Thing If It Ain't Got that Swing" used the sound of a trumpet with a cup mute, "Doo wa, doo wa, doo wa." "Floy doy, floy doy, floy doy" was the nonsense refrain of Slim Gaillard's hit "Flat Foot Floogie with the Floy Floy." Other scat sounds of the 1930s were "za zu za zu," "beedle a di deedle a," "rip dip dip da da," and "wah dee dah dee," which were used to great effect by the vocal trio the Three Keys. Cab Calloway's hit song of 1933, "Zaz Zu Zaz," was even assimilated into the French language with the wartime term "zazou," which meant a guy who dressed in the style of Cab Calloway and acted crazy!

In the 1940s syllables such as "biddle ee bop," "doodle ee bop," "shoo bee doo bee," and "dwee lya bop" permitted the singing of up-tempo eighth-note lines like those of Charlie Parker and Dizzy Gillespie, and gave their style of music its name, bebop. Chet Baker, who became famous for his trumpet playing and singing in the 1950s, used syllables clearly derived from doodle tonguing. Listen to his solo on "But Not for Me" (*Let's Get Lost: The Best of Chet Baker Sings,* Pacific Jazz PCJ B2 92032); he uses the consonants "d" and "b" almost exclusively.

When I started scat singing, I tried using only syllables beginning with "d" and "b," imitating the tonguing and attack of a trumpet or saxophone with "da ba da ba," "doo bee doo bee," etc. After awhile I became comfortable with those sounds, which fit swing and bebop music, but eventually I felt they were limited. I transcribed solos from recordings of two of the greatest jazz singers of all time, Ella Fitzgerald and Sarah Vaughan, and later explored Betty Carter's scatting style.

Ella Fitzgerald's scat syllables fit the bebop style perfectly. She often used "b," "d," "bw" and "dw" with various vowels for a horn-like attack. Her syllables supported the swinging rhythm of her improvised lines and gave her accuracy and flexibility in her up-tempo solos. Dizzy Gillespie composed several tunes made entirely of scat syllables. One of Ella's favorites was a blues called "Ool Ya Koo." Let's look at the syllables of the chorus from Ella's solo on the tune (*Ella Fitzgerald Royal Roost Sessions* with Ray Brown and Trio, Cool 'n' Blue Records, C&B CD112).

She sings the melody twice:

> Blee ya ba doo ool . . . ya, blee ya ba doo ool ya koo,
> Blee ya ba doo ool . . . ya, blee ya ba doo ool ya koo,
> Blee ya ba doo ool . . . ya, blee ya ba doo ool ya koo.

Then she continues with her solo:

> Ooh blee bi bi yoo dee dah doo dee,
> Bah bah buh bi ooh di, di, di,
> 'n deh 'n deh 'n deh
> Doo di di, ow bah 'n di di di, di di yoo, 'n de dleh,
> Eel yah doot 'n di doodle dee, bowm bowm ba biddle ee ooh,
> Bip bee yoo bah bow.

Sarah Vaughan's syllables were integral to her style, matching her smoothly flowing melodic lines. She often started phrases with the consonants "s," "sh" and "z," bringing to mind the sound of brushes on drums that was popular in the "cool jazz" era of the 1950s. You can hear a great example of the "cool" sound of brushes played by drummer Roy Haynes on the recording of Sarah's composition "Shu Lia Bop" (*Sarah*

Vaughan: Swingin' Easy, Emarcy 514 072-2). I recommend transcribing Sarah's scat solo on this song.

Here are the syllables of the first chorus:

Sa lool ya bop, sool ya bop, shool ya bop, shool ya bop,
   shoo bee ooh boo.
Ba dool ya doot 'n, dool ya doot 'n, dool ya doot 'n, doo
   ya doot 'n, doo bee doo.
Sha ga ga dool ya boo bee doo ba doo ba, dee lee ya dee
   'n dee ba ah 'm bee ba ooh 'm bee ba.
Sa whee boo bee deel ya bap 'm, whee ooh bee deel ya
   boo 'm bee bee ooh 'm bee ya.

Betty Carter, one of the great innovators in vocal jazz, added sounds such as "la," "lo" and "le" to the scat vocabulary. This creates a free-flowing mood and fits her favorite device: stretching phrases over the bar lines. She occasionally uses "g" (which can be unwieldy) as an initial consonant, an unusual flavor in an original scat language.

Here's the beginning of her solo on "Surrey with the Fringe on Top" (*Betty Carter at the Village Vanguard,* Verve 519 851-2):

Ah, ah ah leh ah lehdle lodo leh.
Ah do beh beh ha deh ah deh deh deh.
La la ga da go lu la da, ah du dlay bop.

Students often ask me which syllables to use when they improvise. To develop your own vocabulary, the first step is to listen to jazz instruments. Try to imitate a saxophone, a trumpet, a plucked or bowed bass, even percussion and drums. But don't stop there; use those sounds to stimulate your imagination and create your own scat language. Check out Bobby McFerrin—his body percussion and vocal renditions of other instruments are amazing, but his musical creativity transcends mere imitation.

On songs with Brazilian or Latin grooves, syllables such as "shoo bee doo bee" bring to mind the 1930s and 40s, and while they suit the swing and bebop music of their time, they sound out of place on Brazilian songs. Bossa nova, which became popular in America in the 1960s, generally evokes a softer, more romantic, contemplative mood. Try using "l" as a beginning consonant, or the soft consonant sounds "v," "sh" or "z," which are also found in the Portuguese language.

As far as I know, there is no standard way of writing scat syllables. I have consulted two experts in vocal jazz, Darmon Meader, of the group New York Voices, and Bob Stoloff, assistant chair of the vocal department at the Berklee School of Music and author of *Scat!* (Gerard and Sarzin Publishing). Both maintain that no codified system exists, and that composers and arrangers generally invent their own spellings.

During my years of teaching throughout Europe, I've observed that non–English speakers find it difficult to decipher the various spellings of scat syllables. With that in mind, I created the following syllable chart, which lists each vowel or combination of vowels I've used in the audio, the International Phonetic Association symbol for that sound, and an English word containing the same sound.

When I sang the modal workouts for this book, I interpreted the written exercises, as is commonly done in jazz singing, occasionally dividing a syllable over the space of two notes. You'll see this notated as two notes tied with a dotted slur, with the syllable divided beneath them.

Judy Niemack's Pronunciation Guide for Scat Syllables

Written vowels	Equivalent vowels *International Phonetic Association (IPA)* *abbreviation*	English language example
ee	i	b<u>ee</u>
eh	ɛ	b<u>e</u>d
ay	e (or eɪ)	p<u>ay</u>
o	əʊ	n<u>o</u>
oo	u	b<u>oo</u>t
a	ɑ	f<u>a</u>ther
ah (used on held notes, or for separate "ah" syllables)	ɑ:	f<u>a</u>ther (but held longer)
o followed by a consonant other than h	ɑ	shop
aw	ɔ	awe
a followed by a consonant other than h	æ	scat
uh	ʌ	but
i	ɪ	sit
ai	ɑɪ	pie
ow	aʊ	out
u followed by a consonant other than h	ʊ	book
yoo	ju	you

THE MODAL WORKOUTS

For these audio examples I have used B♭ as the starting note for each mode because it provides the best vocal range for the majority of men's and women's voices. However, in the examples at the beginning of each chapter, I have shown the modes in C for easier understanding and comparison.

IONIAN MODE

- The Ionian mode is most commonly known as the major scale.
- The half steps occur between steps 3 and 4 and between steps 7 and 8.
- Since it is the same as the major scale, there are no alterations.

Uses

Because it has a major third and a major seventh, it's the mode used with the major family chords, including the major triad, major seventh chord, and major 6(9) chords. Here are the chord symbols in C that suggest the use of this mode: C, Cmaj7, C6, C6(9), Cmaj9.

Dissonances

In jazz harmony, one note in this scale is commonly called the avoid note. It is the fourth degree of the scale, which is dissonant to the major chord and has a strong tendency to resolve to the third scale degree. This note works well as a passing tone, when sung or played on the weak part of the beat, but sounds dissonant on a strong beat. Notice this dissonance of the fourth note when you sing the interval exercise in the Ionian mode.

When the major seventh is present in the chord, the first or eighth scale step is relatively dissonant and tends to resolve down to the seventh. When we use notes of the scale other than these two dissonant notes (the fourth and the first), we are left with the second, third, fifth, sixth and seventh degrees of the scale. If we start on the fifth and sing the fifth, sixth, seventh, second and third, we have sung a major pentatonic scale, which is an interesting color to use improvising over a major seventh chord. We can also start on the third and sing the third, fifth, sixth, seventh, and second, creating a minor pentatonic scale.

The Ionian mode doesn't work where the harmony contains chromatic alterations, for example with a major 7♯5 or a major 7(♯11) chord.

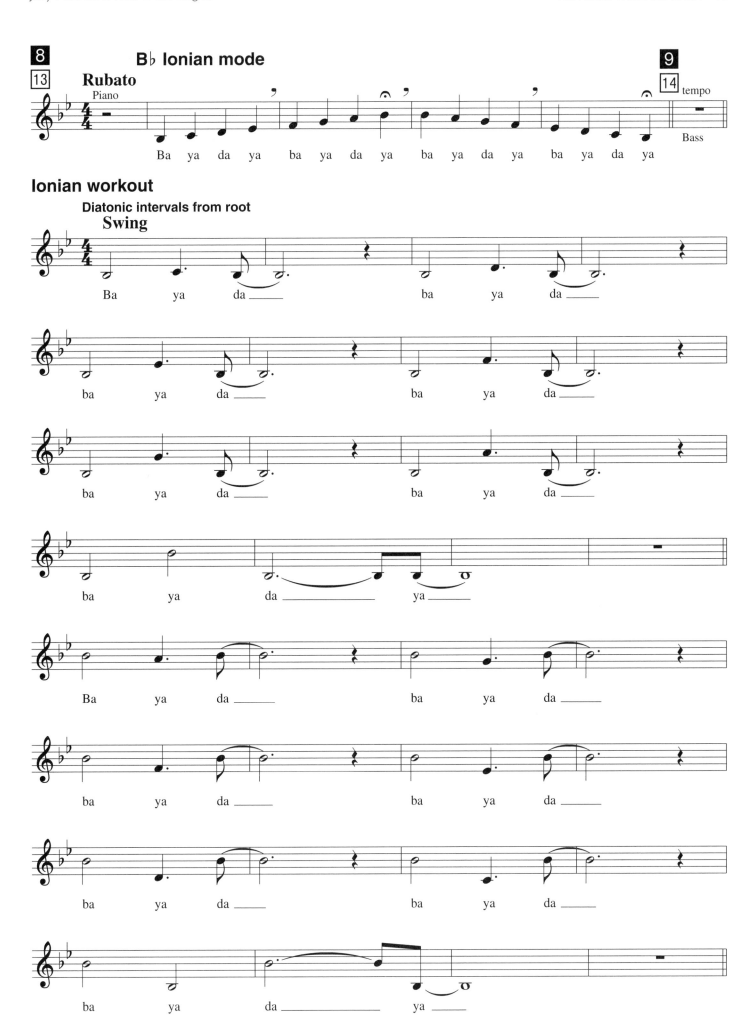

DORIAN MODE

C Dorian

- The Dorian mode is built on the second degree of a major scale, so its parent scale (the scale with which it shares a key signature) is a major second (or whole step) lower.
- The half steps occur between steps 2 and 3 and between steps 6 and 7.
- It can be thought of as a pure minor scale with a raised sixth scale step, or as a major scale with a lowered third and lowered seventh.

Uses

Because it has a minor third and a minor seventh, the Dorian mode is generally used with the minor family chords, including the minor chords that function as **I**, **II** or **V** chords of a major or minor key.

Here are the chords in C that suggest the use of this mode: Cm, Cm6, Cm7, Cm9, Cm11, Cm13.

The Dorian mode is generally used with minor family chords without alterations; for example, it can be used over a **II–V** progression in the key of its parent scale, so that in C major it would be used over a Dm7, G7 progression.

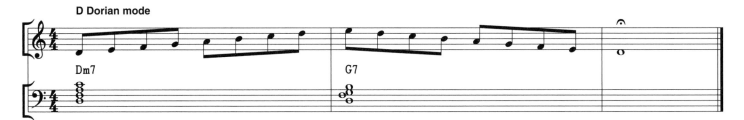

If the minor chord functions as a **III** or **VI** chord, the Phrygian or Aeolian may be a better choice.

Dissonances

In this scale there are no notes dissonant to the harmony, and, in fact, the Dorian scale comprises all the tones of a complete minor 13th chord: D, F, A, C, E, G and B. Although there are no notes to avoid, certain notes may sound better than others when stressed.

The Dorian mode is commonly used in jazz. When Miles Davis and other musicians became fascinated with modal improvisation in the 1950s, they found that the Dorian mode suited their needs. Tunes such as John Coltrane's "Impressions" and Miles Davis's "So What," composed entirely in Dorian mode, remain popular vehicles for improvisation.

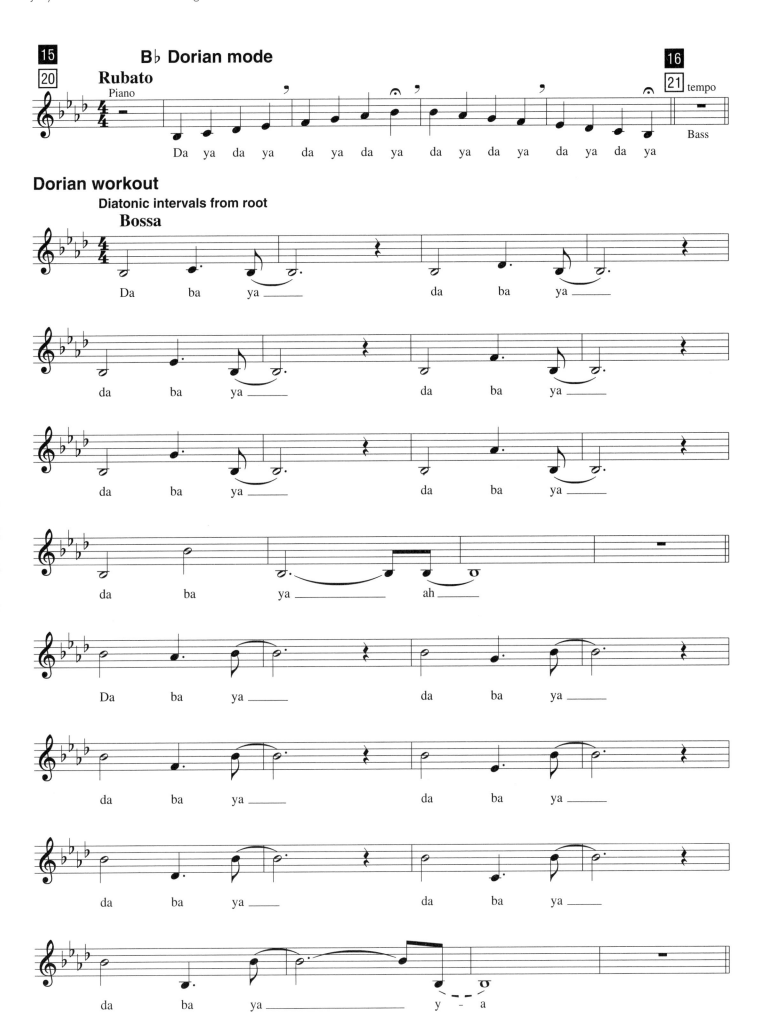

19 **Call and response**

Da ya da ya da ya da ya da ya da ya da ____

Da ya doo ya da doo ya dwee ya ____

Shoo ba doo bay ____ ya doo bay ____ ya doo bow ____

Doo-dle ooh doo-dle ay ya doo yoo day y-a dow ____

Doo da day yo ba doo vay ah dow ____

Shoo va doo vay ooh ya doo vo day ya ____

Shoo doo ba ____ ya doo bay boo dow ____

Phrygian mode

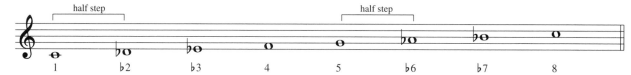

C Phrygian

- The Phrygian mode is built on the third degree of a major scale, so its parent scale is a major third below.
- The half steps occur between steps 1 and 2 and between 5 and 6.
- It can be thought of as a pure minor scale with a lowered second, or a major scale with a lowered second, third, sixth and seventh.

Uses

Because it has a minor third and minor seventh, this mode is generally used with the minor chords that function as the **III** or **VI** chord in a major key, although the Aeolian mode might be a better choice for the **VI** chord.

Here are the chord symbols in C that suggest the use of this mode: Cm, Cm7, C7sus(♭9).

It can also be used in minor keys or in momentary key centers in which the **II** chord is a major seventh chord.

For example, in the following progression, the C Phrygian mode can be used throughout because the **II** chord (D♭maj7) is a half step above the tonic minor seventh (Cm7):

But the Phrygian mode is most often played in compositions written in the Phrygian mode, or with long sections using it. In these cases the chord played is a sus7(♭9) chord. The sus7(♭9) sound was introduced into jazz harmony in the 1960s, in compositions by John Coltrane, Kenny Dorham and Wayne Shorter. Unlike the other chords we've looked at, the sus7(♭9) chord does not include the third, but is usually voiced with the root, flat second (which functions as a ♭9), fourth, fifth and seventh. You will hear this type of chord on the track for the Phrygian mode.

Dissonances

In this scale the second and sixth scale steps are dissonant and want to resolve downward to the first and fifth notes of the scale. For example, in the key of C, the sixth note of the E Phrygian mode is C, which sounds very dissonant against the Em7 chord, and has a tendency to resolve down to the B.

Lydian mode

C Lydian

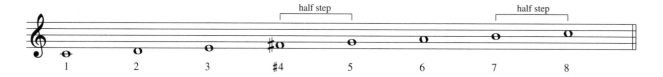

- The Lydian mode is built on the fourth note of a major scale, so its parent scale is located a perfect fourth below.
- The half steps occur between steps 4 and 5 and between 7 and 8.
- It can be thought of as a major scale with a raised fourth.

Uses

The Lydian mode has a major third and major seventh, and is used with the major family chords, especially when there is a #11 or #4 in the harmony. However, it's not necessary to have the #11 present; the scale usually sounds good with major seventh chords as well, since the raised fourth eliminates the naturally dissonant fourth degree, or avoid note. When the major seventh chord functions as a **IV** chord, the Lydian mode should always be used.

Here are the chord symbols in C that suggest the use of this mode: C, Cmaj7, Cmaj7(#11).

Dissonances

As is the case with the Ionian or major scale, when the major seventh is present in the chord, the first or eighth scale step is relatively dissonant and tends to resolve down to the seventh. There are two pentatonic scales which can be used over this mode. If we start on the fifth and sing the fifth, sixth, seventh, second and third, we will create a major pentatonic scale. If we start on the third and sing the third, fifth, sixth, seventh and second, we will create a minor pentatonic scale.

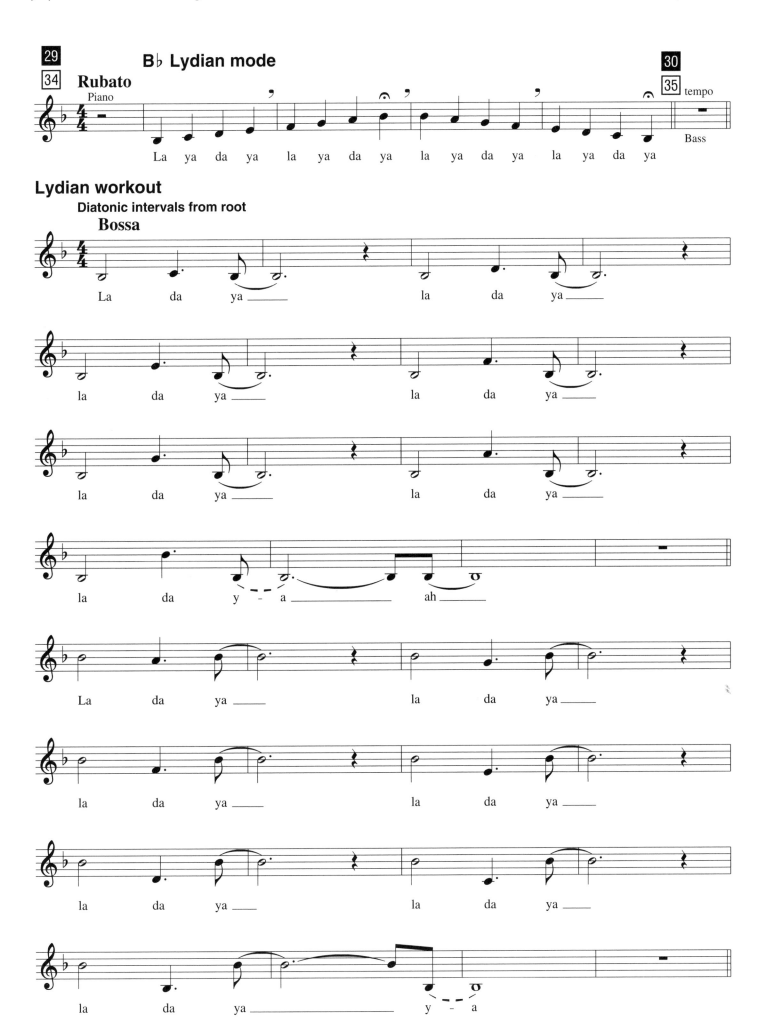

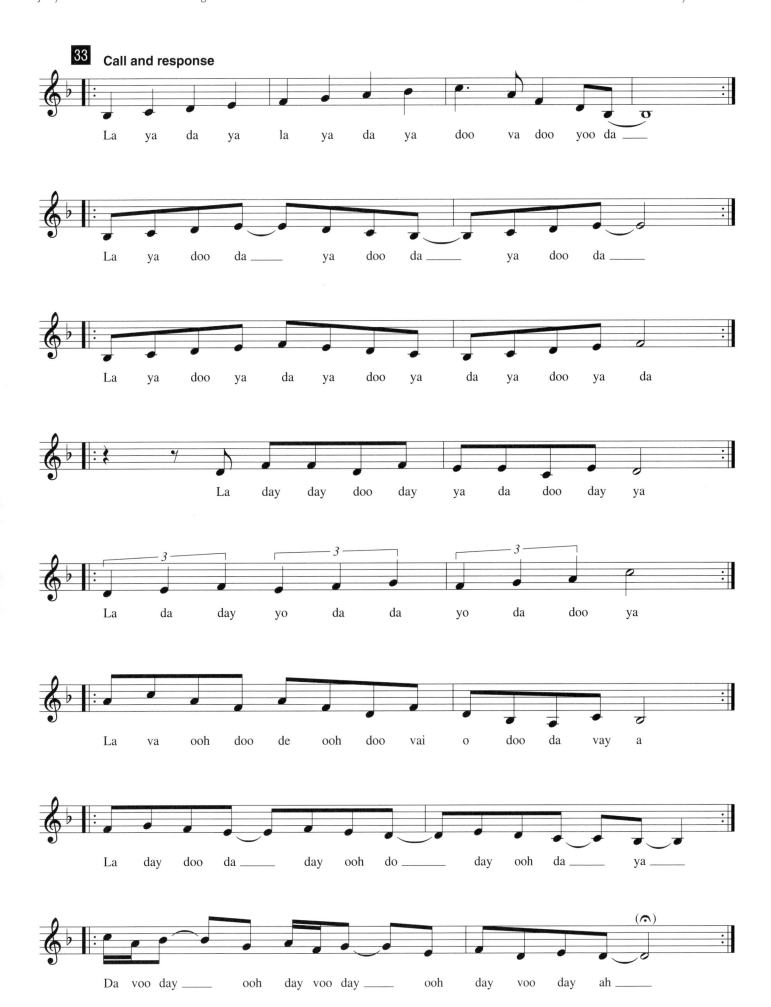

MIXOLYDIAN MODE

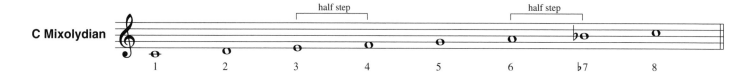

- The Mixolydian mode is also called the dominant scale, because it is built on the fifth note of a major scale. Its parent scale is located a perfect fifth below.
- The half steps occur between steps 3 and 4 and between 6 and 7.
- It can be thought of as a major scale with a lowered seventh.

Uses

Because it contains a major third and a minor seventh, it is used with dominant family harmonies with no alterations, such as the dominant seventh chord.

Here are the chord symbols in C that suggest the use of this mode: C7, C9, C11, C13, Csus7, Csus9, Csus11, Csus13.

The Mixolydian mode is also used when there is a suspended fourth in a dominant seventh chord, as in a C7sus4 chord. The "sus" refers to the suspended fourth degree of the chord (which in C would be F), which replaces the third in the chord. In this case, the fourth step is a stronger choice than the third.

This scale doesn't work when there are chromatic alterations in the harmony, for example, with C7♭5, C7♯5, C7(♯9), or C7(♯11).

Dissonances

In this scale we once again find the avoid note: the fourth scale degree, which is dissonant to the chord and has a strong tendency to resolve to the third degree of the scale. However, when it is emphasized, the resolution has a bluesy sound.

B♭ Mixolydian mode

Mixolydian workout

Diatonic intervals from root

38 **Diatonic thirds**

Doo   day   ah ____   day   y - a   day   ah ____   day   y -

- a   day   ah ____   day   y - a   day   y - a ____

Doo   day   ah ____   day   y - a   day   ah ____   day   y -

a   day   ah ____   day   y - a   day   y - a ____   Doo__

39 **Diatonic triads**

____   way   ooh   doo __   way   ooh __   doo   way   ooh   doo __   way   ooh __

doo   way   ooh   doo __   way   ooh __   doo   way   ooh   doo __   way   doo __

Doo   way   ooh   doo __   way   ooh __   doo   way   ooh   doo __   way   ooh __

doo   way   ooh   doo __   way   ooh __   doo   way   ooh __   ya __

2

40 **Call and response**

AEOLIAN MODE

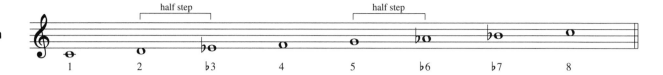

C Aeolian

- The Aeolian mode is also called pure minor, natural minor, or the relative minor of its parent major scale. It is built on the sixth note of a major scale, so its parent scale is a major sixth below (or a minor third above).
- The half steps occur between steps 2 and 3 and between 5 and 6.
- It can be thought of as a pure minor scale, or a major scale with a lowered third, sixth and seventh.

Uses

The Aeolian mode is best used with minor family chords that function as either **III** or **VI** chords in a major key. When a minor chord functions as a **I** or **II** chord, the Dorian mode is usually a better choice.

Here are the chord symbols in C that suggest the use of this mode: Cm, Cm7, Cm9, Cmb6, Cm7(b13).

The Aeolian mode can also be used when a **VIm7** chord in a major key becomes the new minor key center. For example, when the new tonic minor chord, **Im7**, is the same as the old **VIm7** chord of its relative major key (i.e., when the key center shifts from C major to A minor), the Aeolian is appropriate.

It can also be used over a chord built on the second step of a minor key. In the key of D minor, for example, that chord is an Em7 with a lowered fifth.

Therefore, in the following progression the D Aeolian mode is the best choice over the Em7b5 chord.

D Aeolian mode

Dissonances

The sixth step is dissonant to a minor chord and tends to resolve downward to the fifth.

B♭ Aeolian mode

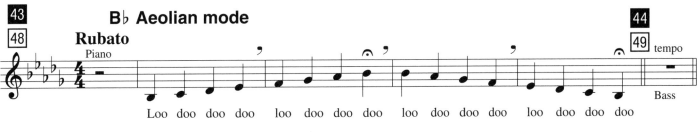

Loo doo doo doo   loo doo doo doo   loo doo doo doo   loo doo doo doo

Aeolian workout

Diatonic intervals from root

La   ya   ya ____   la   da   ya ____

la   da   ya ____   la   da   ya ____

la   da   ya ____   la   da   ya ____

la   da   y - a   y - a

La   da   ya ____   la   da   ya ____

la   da   ya ____   la   da   ya ____

la   da   ya ____   la   da   ya ____

la   da   ya _____   y - a

45 **Diatonic thirds**

La   da   ya ____   la   y - a   da   ya ____   la   y -

- a   da   ya ____   la   y - a   da   ya ____   La __

____   y - a   da __   y - a   la   y - a   da ____   y - a

la   y - a   da ____   y - a   la   y - a   da ____   Y -

46 **Diatonic triads**

- a   da   doo   ya __   da   doo __   ya   da   doo   ya __   da   doo __

ya   da   doo   ya __   da   doo __   ya   da   doo   ya __   da   doo __

Doo   ya   da   doo __   ya   da __   doo   ya   da   doo __   ya   da __

doo   ya   da   doo __   ya   da __   doo   ya   da   ya __

47 Call and response

Da ya da ya da ya da ya da ya da ya da _____

Doo yoo doo ya _____ dai yoo da

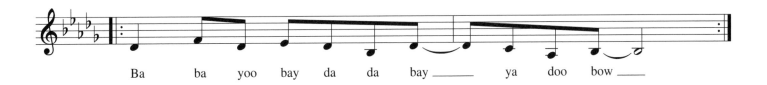

Ba ba yoo bay da da bay _____ ya doo bow _____

Ba ya doo ba ba ya doo ba ba ya doo ya dow

Da ya doo da _____ ya doo da _____ ba ba yow _____

Doo ya doo doo doo doo ba _____

LOCRIAN MODE

C Locrian

- This mode is built on the seventh degree of the major scale, so its parent scale is a major seventh below (or a half step above).
- The half steps occur between steps 1 and 2 and between 4 and 5.
- It can be thought of as a pure minor scale with lowered second and fifth scale steps, or a major scale with lowered second, third, fifth, sixth and seventh.

Uses

Because it has a minor third, a minor fifth and a minor seventh, this mode is generally used with minor chords with a lowered fifth scale degree, or half-diminished chords. This mode differs from the others we've looked at in that all the other modes in the major scale have a perfect fifth, whereas in the Locrian mode the fifth is diminished.

Only one chord suggests the use of this mode: in C, Cm7♭5.

Dissonances

The second degree is dissonant when used with a half-diminished chord. It is this mode's avoid note, which tends to resolve down to the root, or first degree of the scale.

If the Locrian mode is used with a half-diminished chord that includes an unaltered ninth (not flatted or sharped), the second scale step must be raised to avoid dissonance with the unaltered ninth in the harmony. The resulting scale, known as the Locrian ♯2 mode, eliminates the problem of the avoid note, but it is another mode, for another book!

50 **55** **B♭ Locrian mode**

Rubato

La ya da ya la ya da ya la ya da ya la ya da ya

Locrian workout

Diatonic intervals from root

Latin

Ba ya dow___ ba y - a dow___

ba ya dow___ ba ya dow___

ba ya dow___ ba ya dow___

ba ya da_____ y - a

La da ya___ la da ya ___

la da ya ___ la da ya ___

la da ya___ y - a

54 **Call and response**

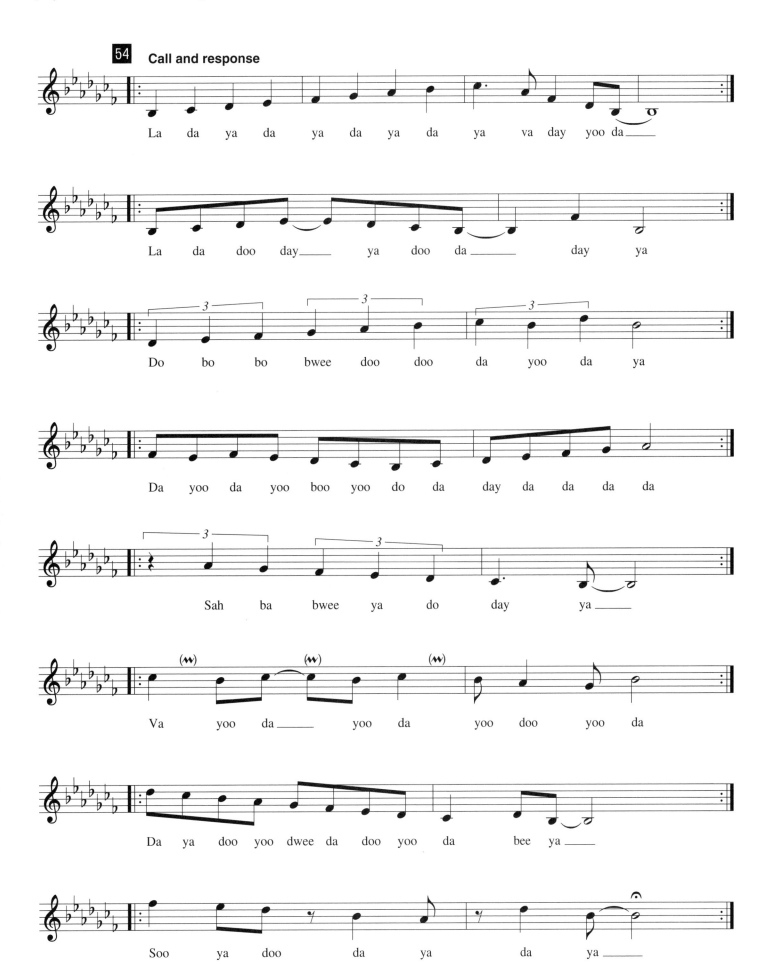

La   da   ya   da   ya   da   ya   da   ya   va   day   yoo   da____

La   da   doo   day____   ya   doo   da _____   day   ya

Do   bo   bo   bwee   doo   doo   da   yoo   da   ya

Da   yoo   da   yoo   boo   yoo   do   da   day   da   da   da   da

Sah   ba   bwee   ya   do   day   ya ____

Va   yoo   da ____   yoo   da   yoo   doo   yoo   da

Da   ya   doo   yoo   dwee   da   doo   yoo   da   bee   ya ____

Soo   ya   doo   da   ya   da   ya ____

HEAR IT AND SING IT! IN THE CLASSROOM

The audio included with this book is designed to be useful in high school and college jazz choir settings, as well as in vocal improvisation classes. The vocal warm-up tracks can be used with the entire group at the beginning of a rehearsal, freeing the teacher to demonstrate good posture, blend and correct breathing techniques. With help from the teacher in pointing out which scales are being sung in the warm-ups (explained in the accompanying text), students will learn to hear the difference between major and minor scales. This will prepare them for the next section, the modal workouts. The workout tracks provide an easy way to introduce the basic tools of vocal improvisation to a group.

Here are some specific ideas for using *Hear It and Sing It!* in the classroom.

Since jazz is not part of today's popular daily listening diet, your students may need some help getting the swing feeling. Adding simple movements to the warm-ups will help them loosen up and feel the rhythm. Start the first warm-up by snapping your fingers on the second and fourth beats, and ask the students to do the same. Then add a simple movement, shifting your weight from side to side, or stepping to the right and left (step, snap, step, snap) in time to the music.

After warming up with tracks 1–7, ask everyone to stand in a circle with you. Play track 8, explaining the Ionian mode, pointing out that it is commonly known as the major scale, and where the half steps occur. Then play track 8 again, asking the students to sing along. Tell them that the next section (track 9) will include exercises and patterns using the Ionian mode. While it plays, illustrate with hand gestures the shapes and directions of each pattern. After only a few repetitions, the workouts, which follow the same patterns in each mode, will become familiar to the students and they will remember them without the hand motions.

After the call-and-response section, play track 13 continuing on to track 14 (rhythm section alone), and improvise two-measure phrases using the Ionian mode for them to repeat. Repeat the phrase until everyone can sing it back to you. Next, ask for a volunteer to be the leader and sing a few two-measure phrases with the track for the group to repeat. If he can't think of anything, he can copy one of the phrases I've sung and build on it or vary it. By repeating the short melodic motives in the call-and-response exercises and using them as themes to develop, the students will begin to create their own melodic vocabularies. At the same time, they'll become familiar with commonly used scat syllables, and more comfortable improvising in front of their peers.

The only rule of this improvisation "game" is that the leader must remember what he sang, and repeat it until everyone in the group can sing it. Encourage them to begin with a simple phrase. Even singing one or two different notes with a clear rhythmic pattern is enough. In this way your students will learn to hear and improvise with the scales while hearing the chords, while developing their musical memories.

I've found it most effective to practice only one mode in each rehearsal, so that the students get acquainted with it before moving to the next. Repetition is key, and it may take a few weeks for them to become comfortable with new scale sounds. For beginning improvisers I recommend learning the modes in this order: Ionian, Lydian, Mixolydian, Dorian, Aeolian, Phrygian, Locrian.

If you, the teacher, have fun with the exercises and convey the message that vocal improvisation is a creative journey, where "wrong notes" are not a crime, the students will be free to try new things and learn from their mistakes without thinking they are "wrong." The balance between being aware of what note you are singing and freely improvising is a delicate one, and requires lots of practice with the scale sounds. It's important to create a situation where the student can be successful from the beginning—for example, by repeating a simple phrase or making up a short phrase for the others to sing back. For the student, your relaxed acceptance of the effort and encouragement to try it again are among the most important elements in the learning process.

———————————

Now that you've learned the seven modes of the major scale, reviewed the basics of music theory, and read about the history of scat syllables and modal improvisation, you're well on your way to the next step: improvising over chord progressions.

I hope this method has helped you to understand the how and why of modal improvisation, to identify and sing the modes and to enjoy your own exploration of modal jazz. Good luck with your future musical adventures!

Judy Niemack

ABOUT JUDY NIEMACK

"If you want to know what real jazz singing can be (but rarely is) listen to Judy Niemack. . . . She is a musician in the truest sense."

Dan Morgenstern
Down Beat

"Her dynamically delivered three-octave vocals soar above superb accompaniment."

Nancy Ann Lee
Jazz Times

". . . one of the best, and purest jazz singers ever . . . a voice with the clarity of a mountain stream, accuracy of pitch and time that is a wonder to hear, perfect diction and sensitivity to lyrics . . . a disciplined improvisational gift that makes her scat-sung lines music."

Safford Chamberlain
L.A. Jazz Scene

Singer Judy Niemack is a consummate artist, both as a vocalist and a musician. She explores jazz improvisation like a virtuoso horn player, with a modern approach to the standards. Her scatting and delivery of lyrics come straight out of the jazz tradition, while she breaks new ground with her original lyrics and songs.

Niemack was born in Pasadena, California, where she began to study classical voice at 17. At 18, High School friends who studied improvisation with the great tenor saxophonist Warne Marsh introduced her to him, and she became fascinated with jazz. Continuing her classical studies at the New England Conservatory in Boston and at the Cleveland Institute of Music, she soon realized that her true path lay in improvised music. She returned to California, where she sang in jazz clubs at night and studied improvisation by day. She was Marsh's only vocal student, and he taught her as if she was a horn player. When she moved to New York City in 1977, her first major engagement was a week at the Village Vanguard with Marsh. Judy has subsequently toured and taught throughout the USA, Asia and Europe. Her next recording will be released on Sunnyside Records in 2022, featuring guitarist Peter Bernstein and pianist Sullivan Fortner.

She currently divides her time between Berlin and New York City. As Germany's first professor of Jazz Voice, she headed the jazz vocal department at the Hanns Eisler Music Conservatory (now the Jazz Institut Berlin) for 25 years and for 13 years was Professor of Vocal Jazz at Musikene, the Higher Music School of the Basque Country in Spain.

She has recorded fourteen CDs as a leader, with such jazz luminaries as Kenny Barron, Joey Baron, Ray Drummond, Billy Hart, Fred Hersch, Joe Lovano, Jim McNeely, Adam Nussbaum, Toots Thielemans, Mal Waldron, Cedar Walton and Kenny Werner.

Niemack has written and recorded several of her own songs, and has added lyrics to jazz standards, many of which are available online at https://jazzleadsheets.com/composers/judy-niemack.html. She has also written lyrics for compositions by Richie Beirach, Clifford Brown, Kenny Dorham, Bill Evans, Sonny Stitt, Lee Konitz, Pat Metheny, Thelonious Monk, Kirk Nurock, Richie Powell, Eric Alexander, Peter Bernstein and Mike Stern, among others.

DISCOGRAPHY

AS A LEADER

By Heart featuring Warne Marsh, Eddie Gomez (Seabreeze, 1978)

Blue Bop featuring Cedar Walton, Curtis Fuller, Ray Drummond, Joey Baron (Freelance, 1988)

Long as You're Living featuring Joe Lovano, Fred Hersch, Billy Hart (Freelance, 1990)

Heart's Desire with Kenny Barron (Stash, 1991)

Straight Up featuring Toots Thielemans, Kenny Werner, Adam Nussbaum, Mark Feldman, Jeanfrançois Prins (Freelance, 1993)

Mingus, Monk and Mal duet with Mal Waldron (Freelance, 1994)

. . . Night and the Music featuring Kenny Werner, Jeanfrançois Prins, Ray Drummond, Billy Hart, Eric Friedlander (Freelance, 1996)

About Time featuring Eddie Gomez, Jeanfrançois Prins, Lee Konitz, David Friedman, Edson da Silva (Café) (Sony Jazz, 2003)

Jazz Singer's Practice Session featuring Fred Hersch, Scott Colley, Dick Weller (GAM, 2003)

Blue Nights featuring Don Sickler, Gary Bartz, Jim McNeely, Jeanfrancois Prins, Dennis Irwin, Victor Lewis (Blujazz, 2007)

In the Sundance featuring Bruce Barth, Jeanfrancois Prins, Rufus Reid, Bruno Castellucci (Blujazz, 2009)

Listening To You featuring Dan Tepfer (Sunnyside 2017)

New York Stories featuring Jim McNeely & The Danish Radio Big Band (Sunnyside, 2018)

Sing Your Song with Wolfgang Koehler (Contemplate Music, 2019)

AS A GUEST (SELECTED DISCOGRAPHY)

Beauty and the Prince with Jeanfrançois Prins featuring Fred Hersch, Hein van de Geyn, Bruno Castellucci (AMC, 1993)

Rhapsody Volumes 1 and 2 with Lee Konitz (Paddle Wheel, 1993)

The Other Side of Walter Boeykens (distributed by Sony, 1994)

For more information, visit www.judyniemack.com.

ACKNOWLEDGMENTS

Text editor: Jessica Raimi

Music editors: Don Sickler and Gloria Cooper, Ed.D.

Cover photos and cover design: Terry Chamberlain

Book design: Maureen Sickler

Music engraving: Osho Endo

Photograph of Ms. Niemack: Philippe Fresco

Photograph of piano keys: Jeanfrançois Prins

Hear It and Sing It! audio

Judy Niemack, voice

Bruce Barth, piano

Dennis Irwin, bass

Kenny Washington, drums

Produced by Judy Niemack and Jeanfrançois Prins.

Recorded and mixed by Michael Brorby at Acoustic Recording in
Brooklyn, N.Y., and by Jeanfrançois Prins at PH Studio in Berlin.

Special thanks to Bruce, Dennis and Kenny for playing music that
makes us want to sing, Jeanfrançois for his support, advice and extreme
musicality, Jessica for her patience and great interest in this project,
Ashley Kahn (author of *The Making of "Kind of Blue"*), Yuko Fujiyama,
Dan Haerle, Peter Tenner, Mark Levine, Matthias Hessel, Patti Dunham,
Marty Elkins, Don Sickler, Maureen Sickler, and students at the Hanns
Eisler Hochschule für Musik in Berlin.

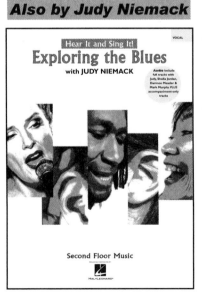